TRAVEL MATH

MATH 24/7

BANKING MATH

BUSINESS MATH

COMPUTER MATH

CULINARY MATH

FASHION MATH

GAME MATH

SHOPPING MATH

SPORTS MATH

TIME MATH

TRAVEL MATH

MATH 24/7

TRAVEL MATH

HELEN THOMPSON

Mason Crest

Mason Crest
450 Parkway Drive, Suite D
Broomall, PA 19008
www.masoncrest.com

Printed in the United States of America.

First printing
9 8 7 6 5 4 3 2 1

Series ISBN: 978-1-4222-2901-9
ISBN: 978-1-4222-2911-8
ebook ISBN: 978-1-4222-8922-8

Cataloging-in-Publication Data on file with the Library of Congress.

Produced by Vestal Creative Services.
www.vestalcreative.com

Contents

INTRODUCTION

How would you define math? It's not as easy as you might think. We know math has to do with numbers. We often think of it as a part, if not the basis, for the sciences, especially natural science, engineering, and medicine. When we think of math, most of us imagine equations and blackboards, formulas and textbooks.

But math is actually far bigger than that. Think about examples like Polykleitos, the fifth-century Greek sculptor, who used math to sculpt the "perfect" male nude. Or remember Leonardo da Vinci? He used geometry—what he called "golden rectangles," rectangles whose dimensions were visually pleasing—to create his famous *Mona Lisa*.

Math and art? Yes, exactly! Mathematics is essential to disciplines as diverse as medicine and the fine arts. Counting, calculation, measurement, and the study of shapes and the motions of physical objects: all these are woven into music and games, science and architecture. In fact, math developed out of everyday necessity, as a way to talk about the world around us. Math gives us a way to perceive the real world—and then allows us to manipulate the world in practical ways.

For example, as soon as two people come together to build something, they need a language to talk about the materials they'll be working with and the object that they would like to build. Imagine trying to build something—anything—without a ruler, without any way of telling someone else a measurement, or even without being able to communicate what the thing will look like when it's done!

The truth is: We use math every day, even when we don't realize that we are. We use it when we go shopping, when we play sports, when we look at the clock, when we travel, when we run a business, and even when we cook. Whether we realize it or not, we use it in countless other ordinary activities as well. Math is pretty much a 24/7 activity!

And yet lots of us think we hate math. We imagine math as the practice of dusty, old college professors writing out calculations endlessly. We have this idea in our heads that math has nothing to do with real life, and we tell ourselves that it's something we don't need to worry about outside of math class, out there in the real world.

But here's the reality: Math helps us do better in many areas of life. Adults who don't understand basic math applications run into lots of problems. The Federal Reserve, for example, found that people who went bankrupt had an average of one and a half times more debt than their income—in other words, if they were making $24,000 per year, they had an average debt of $36,000. There's a basic subtraction problem there that should have told them they were in trouble long before they had to file for bankruptcy!

As an adult, your career—whatever it is—will depend in part on your ability to calculate mathematically. Without math skills, you won't be able to become a scientist or a nurse, an engineer or a computer specialist. You won't be able to get a business degree—or work as a waitress, a construction worker, or at a checkout counter.

Every kind of sport requires math too. From scoring to strategy, you need to understand math—so whether you want to watch a football game on television or become a first-class athlete yourself, math skills will improve your experience.

And then there's the world of computers. All businesses today—from farmers to factories, from restaurants to hair salons—have at least one computer. Gigabytes, data, spreadsheets, and programming all require math comprehension. Sure, there are a lot of automated math functions you can use on your computer, but you need to be able to understand how to use them, and you need to be able to understand the results.

This kind of math is a skill we realize we need only when we are in a situation where we are required to do a quick calculation. Then we sometimes end up scratching our heads, not quite sure how to apply the math we learned in school to the real-life scenario. The books in this series will give you practice applying math to real-life situations, so that you can be ahead of the game. They'll get you started—but to learn more, you'll have to pay attention in math class and do your homework. There's no way around that.

But for the rest of your life—pretty much 24/7—you'll be glad you did!

1
BUYING
PLANE TICKETS

Lee's family is taking a vacation. They are going all the way to Australia! Lee has never even been out of the country before, so he's really looking forward to his first international trip.

Lee and his family have been saving up money for a long time in order to go on this trip. Lee can't remember taking any big vacations, because his family has always dreamed of going to Australia. The plane tickets alone will be expensive. The family has to go during summer, because that's when Lee and his sister have a long break from school. Summer is also when plane tickets tend to cost the most.

They haven't bought the tickets yet, because they're waiting for a good deal. Lee and his mom check online every day for the best price they can find. There will be four people going—Lee, his mom, his dad, and his sister Linda. See if you can find the best deal for Lee's family on the next page.

When Lee and his mom search for flights online, this is what they see:

	Airline A	Airline B	Airline C	Airline D
Non-stop	1,829.99	1818.80	N/A	1818.80
One-stop	1651.79	1805.80	1639.80	1818.50

Nonstop flights will leave right from the airport right in Los Angeles, where Lee and his family live, and arrive in Sydney, Australia. Flights with one stop have a layover along the way, which adds a few hours to the trip.

Lee's family has two things to think about: how much can they afford to spend on tickets, and how fast do they want to get to Australia?

1. Which flights are cheaper, nonstop or one-stop?

2. Which flights do you think would be shorter, nonstop or one-stop? Why?

    Lee's family decides to save money and have a longer flight, so they look at one-stop flights.

3. What is the difference in prices between Airline A's one-stop flight and Airline C's one-stop flight?

Airline A offers a discount on tickets for young people under 18. Both Lee and Linda are under 18, so their plane tickets would cost 25% less.

Percents are ways of saying "parts out of 100." So 25% is 25 parts out of a hundred. To figure out what 25% of the plane ticket's price is, you can convert the percentage into a decimal number by moving the decimal point two places to the left. Then 25% becomes .25. Next, multiply the number the first number by the decimal:

4. $1651.79 x .25 =

You have just found what the discount on the ticket price was. You still need to find out what the total price with the discount is. Just subtract the discount from the original price.

5. What is the discounted ticket price?

6. How much will the plane tickets be all together, for the whole family?

2
BUDGETING

Now that Lee's family has bought the plane tickets, they can figure out how much the rest of their trip will cost. They spent a lot of money on the tickets, so they have less now in their savings. Now they will create a budget, which is a list of things they can spend money on, along with how much money they can spend.

Everyone in the family has something they want to do. Lee wants to go snorkeling. Linda wants to go to a beach (even though July will be winter in Australia because it is in the southern **hemisphere**). Lee's dad wants to go to an art museum. And Lee's mom wants to go out for a nice dinner.

Most of the things they want to do will cost money. They also have to pay for a hotel, buy food, and rent a car or take buses around the country. Making a budget before they go will help them know how much they will be spending on their vacation.

Here is a list of all the things on which Lee's family will be spending money:

hotel room: $175/night
food: $15/day per person
nice dinner: $25/person
snorkeling: $20/person
beach: free
museum: $10/adult; $7/child under 18
transportation: $300 for whichever kind of transportation they decide to use

1. Fill out the same chart, but with the costs multiplied out to account for all 4 people. They are staying in Australia for 8 days and 7 nights:

   hotel room:
   food:
   nice dinner:
   snorkeling:
   beach:
   museum:
   transportation:

2. What is the total they will spend in Australia? What is their total including airfare?

Over the past few years, Lee's parents have put aside $7500 for the trip. The family has also started a piggy bank at home to save their spare change for the trip. Right now, the piggy bank has $87.75.

3. Does the family have enough money for the whole trip? If not, how much more will they have to save to pay for the whole thing?

4. The trip is still 4 months away. How much will the family need to save each month in order to have enough for their trip?

3
LUGGAGE SIZE

Lee's trip to Australia has finally arrived! They leave tomorrow, so Lee is finishing up his packing tonight. The trouble is, he can only pack so much. He wants to bring a lot with him, like clothes, games, travel books, and more. However, the airline they are flying on has limits on the size and weight of the luggage they bring. Lee has to make sure he doesn't go over the limits, or his family will have to pay extra or even leave the luggage behind!

With the help of a scale and a ruler, Lee can make sure his luggage isn't too big or too heavy. The rest of his family members have to do the same thing. See how he figures it out on the next page.

The airline only allows passengers to bring one carry-on bag, one personal item (like a small backpack or purse) and one **checked** bag that goes inside the plane in a separate compartment. Passengers have to pay for any more bags. The airline also has limits on the size of those three things. Here are the limits:

Carry-on:
Cannot be more than 22 inches long, 14 inches wide, and 9 inches tall.
All dimensions added together cannot be more than 45 inches

Personal item:
Cannot exceed 36 inches in length, width, or height

Checked bag:
All dimensions added together cannot be more than 62 inches
Must be 50 pounds or less

Lec measures the suitcase he picks out to take with him as a checked bag. It is 28 inches long, 16 inches wide, and 13 inches tall.

1. How big is the suitcase when its dimensions are added together? Can he bring it with him?

Next, he weighs the suitcase with everything in it. It weighs 52 pounds, which is more than the limit. He has to take something out. He looks in his suitcase and decides he could leave these things behind:

extra video game, 10 ounces
extra pair of jeans, 1 pound, 2 ounces
hiking boots, 2 pounds, 5 ounces
magazine, 6 ounces
extra shirt, 15 ounces

He doesn't need to leave all these things at home, just some of them. (Remember, there are 16 ounces in a pound.)

2. What is one combination of things could he take out of his suitcase to get it under 50 pounds?

Lee has a choice of 2 bags to bring as carry-ons. One is 25 inches long, 13 inches wide, and 8 inches tall. The other is 21 inches long, 14 inches wide, and 8 inches tall.

3. Which one can he bring with him?

Los Angeles London Shanghai Tokyo

New York Moscow New Delhi Sydney

4
TIME ZONE TRAVEL

Lee will be flying through several time zones to get to Australia from Los Angeles. When it is one time in Los Angeles, it will be earlier in Australia.

How can time be different? Time is just how we measure the movement of the sun (or really, the measure of how fast the Earth goes around the sun). In general, we say that it is noon when the sun is at its highest point in the sky. But at different places on the earth, the sun will be at its highest point at different times. Right now, it might be noon where you live. But on the opposite side of the world, it will be dark. Instead of saying that it's noon over there, we adjust time so that it will be noon when the sun is high in the sky there too.

We end up creating time zones. Every few hundred miles you travel, it gets an hour earlier. So if it is 3:00 PM where you are now, a few hundred miles to your west it is 2:00 PM. And a few hundred miles to your east, it is 4:00 PM, because the time is ahead of you to the east. Time doesn't change when you go north or south, though.

Lee is traveling pretty far, and time will change a lot. In order not to get too confused, he'll have to figure out what time it will be at different points in his trip.

Lee and his family are leaving at 8:30 AM on Sunday morning. Their flight takes 13 hours.

They first stop in Auckland, New Zealand for a 1-hour and 30-minute layover. The time difference between Los Angeles and Auckland is +20 hours. In other words, when it is 1:00 AM in Los Angeles, it would be 9:00 PM in Auckland.

Then they fly from Auckland to Sydney, Australia. The flight is 3 hours and 30 minutes long. The time difference between Auckland and Sydney is –2 hours. When it is 9:00 PM in Auckland, it would be 7:00 PM in Sydney. Another way of thinking about it is that Sydney is 18 hours ahead of Los Angeles. When it is 1:00 AM in Los Angeles, it is 7:00 PM in Sydney.

To figure out the first part of their trip, add 13 hours to their departure time, which is 9:30 PM Los Angeles time.

Now convert Los Angeles time into Auckland time:

$$9:30 \text{ PM Sunday} + 20 \text{ hours} = 5:30 \text{ PM Monday}$$

You end up adding so many hours that you change days!

Now try it yourself for the next part of the trip.

1. What time do they fly out of Auckland after their layover (in Auckland time)?

2. What time is it in Auckland when they land?

   Now adjust the time for Sydney by subtracting 2 hours.

3. What time is it Sydney when they finally land?

4. What time and day would it be in Los Angeles when they land in Sydney?

5
AVERAGE SPEED

After the plane takes off, Lee can watch what's going on with the plane on the TV screen in front of him. The screen shows how fast the plane is going and how high it is flying. The plane is flying a lot faster than Lee has ever gone before!

At first, the plane doesn't go very fast, but then it speeds up. By the end of the flight, it starts to slow down again. Lee can calculate the average speed of the plane if he has a little information. He definitely has enough time, since his flight is 13 hours long!

Lee collects some **data** on the flight's speed. Every half an hour, he writes down the speed of the plane. He only starts after the fasten-seatbelt signs are taken down, and the plane is cruising. He is looking for something called the average cruise speed, since he isn't including data on the takeoff and landing speeds.

He makes a chart like this for the first 6 hours (not including a half hour at the beginning for takeoff):

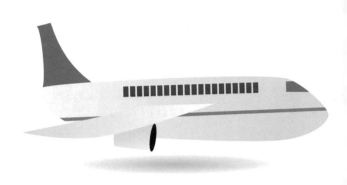

Time	Speed
0 hours	467 mph (miles per hour)
½ hour	489 mph
1 hour	504 mph
1 ½ hours	497 mph
2 hours	512 mph
2 ½ hours	507 mph
3 hours	516 mph
3 ½ hours	521 mph
4 hours	509 mph
4 ½ hours	509 mph
5 hours	513 mph

You can find the average of these speeds by adding them all up and dividing by the number of speeds you added.

1. What is the average speed for the first 6 hours of Lee's flight?

If you know the distance of the flight and the length of the flight, you can also figure out the average distance traveled per hour. Just divide the distance by the number of hours flying.

The distance between Los Angeles and Auckland (where Lee will have a layover) is about 6,520 miles.

2. What is the average speed if you find it this way? Is it close to the other speed you calculated? If not, why might it be different?

6
MONEY EXCHANGE

Once Lee and his family finally land in Australia, they have to exchange their money. All they have are US dollars, but in Australia, no one uses those. Instead, they use the Australian dollar. They will have to exchange their US dollars for Australian dollars before they can spend any money.

The airport has a **currency** exchange booth, where travelers can convert any money they have into Australian dollars. Lee brought along some spending money he wants to exchange. His family also will exchange some of their money for Australian dollars. See how it's done on the next page.

When they get to Australia, Lee sees that 1 US dollar equals 0.95 Australian dollars (sometimes shown as A$). Lee has $80 he has saved and brought with him to spend on whatever he wants. To figure out how many Australian dollars he can get, you just need to multiply the U.S. dollars by the conversion rate, which is .95.

1. How many Australian dollars is US$80 worth?

However, he also sees that the currency exchange booth charges a 10% fee for changing money. They will take 10% of the original amount a customer wants to change.
   First figure out how many U.S. dollars Lee will have to exchange after he pays the fee.

2. How many U.S. dollars will he have to exchange?

Then multiply that amount by the exchange rate to see how many Australian dollars he will have.

3. What is the final amount of Australian currency Lee will have?

Lee's parents have $600 in cash with them. They just want to exchange enough to get them to the hotel. They'll be able to find a currency-exchange business that charges a lower fee once they are out of the airport.

4. How many Australian dollars will they get if they exchange 50 U.S. dollars?

Later on, if they are left with any money at the end of the trip, they will want to change it back to U.S. dollars. This time, they need to know that 1 Australian dollar equals 1.05 U.S. dollars.

5. If they have A$100 at the end of the trip, how many U.S. dollars can they get back with the same fee?

7
TRAVEL
SCHEDULES

Lee and his family are ready to head into the city and start their vacation! To leave the airport and get to their hotel, they will need to take the train and then **transfer** to a bus. They find the train station at the airport, and look around for the schedule.

They take a look at the schedules, and have to figure out how to line them up so the timing works. They're carrying a lot of stuff, so they don't want to end up waiting for a long time in between the train and bus. Check out the schedules on the next page and see if you can figure out the best route for them to take.

They will be taking the train, getting off, and waiting for a bus that also happens to stop at the station they got off at. The train schedule looks like this:

9:06
9:35
10:06
10:35
11:15
12:15
1:15

And the bus schedule looks like this:

9:07
9:37
10:07
10:37
11:07
11:37
12:07
12:37
1:07

Right now it is 9:04. It will take them about 3 minutes to walk to the train platform, but Linda and Lee's dad have to use the restroom first, which will take a few more minutes.

1. Will they make it to the 9:06 train?

2. The train ride lasts 26 minutes. If they take the 9:35 train, which bus can they take?

3. Will they wait more than 5 minutes for the bus? If so, how long?

4. If the bus ride to the hotel takes 16 minutes, and they have to walk another 4 minutes, at what time will they finally get to the hotel?

8
RENTING A CAR

The next morning, Lee is ready to go. His body isn't really sure what time it is, because of all the time changes. But traveling for so many hours was exhausting, and he didn't have any problem getting to sleep.

Everyone spends the next two days walking around Sydney and sightseeing. They go to the museum Lee's dad wanted to visit. They eat a nice dinner, like Lee's mom wanted. But they'll have to wait to snorkel and go to the beach, because they'll have to leave the city.

First thing after breakfast on the third day, Lee's parents want to rent a car. It will be a lot easier to drive out to the beaches and snorkeling, rather than taking the train. They go to a couple places to figure out the best car rental deal. See what they find on the next page.

Lee's parents want to rent the car for two days: the rest of today and tomorrow.

The car rental office has a few choices for them. They can get a very small car with only 2 doors for $19.95 a day. They could get a medium-sized car for $26.95 a day. Or they could get an SUV for $35.95 a day.

1. What will the total cost be for each car for two days?

Lee's parents decide on the medium-sized car, so it fits them all and the stuff they're bringing with them.

The car rental company also offers a GPS rental for $11. Lee thinks that's a good idea so they don't get lost. His parents add that on to the rental.

Finally, the car rental company also charges $15 for insurance.

2. How much will they be paying?

It turns out that the car rental company also charges extra fees. Lee and his family are allowed to drive the rental car 100 miles for free. After that, they have to pay and additional $.10 a mile.

The beach they want to go to today is 38 miles from their hotel. And their hotel is 1.5 miles from the car rental office.

3. If they drive to the beach and back today, how many free miles will they have left to use tomorrow?

Tomorrow they plan on going snorkeling, which means they will be driving out of the city again. The snorkeling tour is just 15 miles from their hotel.

4. Will they end up going over their free mileage limit? If so, by how much and how much will they have to pay?

9
GAS MILEAGE

On the road in Australia, a lot of things seem strange to Lee. Everyone drives on the left side of the road, not like the United States, where everyone drives on the right side. The steering wheel is on the right side, instead of the left. The signs for gas prices also look different—they seem too expensive, but then Lee realizes that Australians must measure their gas in different **units**.

Lee's family will have to figure it out. Besides the fee for renting the car, Lee's family will have to pay for the gas to get them to their destinations. They have to return the car to the rental office with a full tank of gas, so the next customers can take it out right away.

Lee and his family aren't driving very far, but they will be using some gas, and they will have to fill the tank back up. You can do some quick calculations to determine how much gas they will need and how much they will have to spend.

These facts will be useful:

$$1 \text{ gallon} = 3.79 \text{ litres}$$
$$1 \text{ litre} = .264 \text{ gallons}$$

Lee has already used the car's GPS to find how far away his family's driving destinations are. They will drive 38 miles to get to the beach the first day they have the car. (Plus they drove 1.5 miles from the car rental office to the hotel.)

To calculate gas mileage, which is how much gas a car uses while driving a certain distance, you will need to know both the distance and the amount of gas the car used.

In Australia, gas is measured in litres. In the United States, it is measured in gallons. The gas **gauge** in the car shows that they used up about 6 litres of gas.

The equation for gas mileage is:

$$\text{miles traveled} \div \text{gas used}$$

1. What is the gas mileage for their trip in miles-per-litre?

Australians usually **express** mileage in litres per 100 kilometers. To get that number, you have to flip the above equation around and replace the units:

$$\text{litres used} \div \text{kilometers traveled (in fractions of 100)}$$

2. Solve for the mileage on Lee's trip:

$$6 \text{ litres} \div .775 =$$

Lee sees a sign that advertises gas for 137.9. In Australia, fuel is sold in cents per liter. In the United States, it is sold in dollars per gallon. You will need to do some more math to figure out how much the gas to replace their drive will be.

Just multiply the number of litres they have used so far by the price per litre. To get the amount they will pay in dollars, move the decimal point in your answer two spaces to the left.

3. How much will they pay to replace the gas they used up that day?

10
TRANSPORTATION DECISIONS

After their first day driving the car out of the city to go to the beach, Lee's family returns to the hotel. They're pretty exhausted, but they want to go get some dinner and see more of the city. This is their only chance to visit Australia, after all!

Lee really wants to go watch some fireworks out on the water. (Sydney is on the ocean.) The fireworks start at 8:00 PM, and it is 6:00 right now. They figure it'll take about an hour to eat, leaving them an hour to get to the harbor.

But how should they get there? They still have the car. It would be a lot faster to drive—they know where they're going by now, so they probably won't get lost. They could also take a bus to get there, which might take more time. In the end, Lee does some calculations to see which option will be least expensive and will get them to the harbor on time.

One thing they have to think about is the cost of each. How much will gas cost versus how much will they pay for public transportation?

The harbor is 9 miles away according to the GPS. How much will the gas they are using round trip cost? Assume they will pay 137.9/litre. Use the information in the last section to figure out how much gas they will use, and how much it will cost.

1. How many litres of gas will they use? How much will it cost to replace the gas?

   They will also have to pay for parking, which will be $10.

2. How much will they have to pay in total if they drive, including parking and gas?

3. A bus ticket will cost $2.50 per person, per ride. How much will 4 round trip tickets on the bus cost them?

They also have to think about the time. They have an hour to get to the harbor before the fireworks start. The GPS tells them they can drive to the harbor in current traffic in 35 minutes. Lee thinks they should add 10 minutes on to make sure they find parking.

Meanwhile, the bus stop is a 3-minute walk from the hotel. The bus ride will take 40 minutes. The bus stop at the harbor is about a 15-minute walk from where they need to be to see the fireworks.

4. How long will it take to get to the harbor if they drive? What about if they take the bus?

5. Which transportation option do you think they should take? Why?

11
USING A MAP

O n the second day, the GPS in the car breaks. Lee and his family will have to use a map to get to the snorkeling company. They are only driving 15 minutes away, so it's not too hard to get there.

Lee has time to study the map as they drive. He doesn't know much about Australia, so he looks at the big Australian map that came in the car. He's curious about how big Australia is. He has a good idea about how big Los Angeles, California, and the United States are, but he's not sure about Australia.

The map has a key at the bottom, which tells what all the map symbols mean. A big dot, for example, is a big city. The key also has a distance **scale**. A map is a shrunken-down representation of the Earth. Everything on the map is **proportional** to how it is in real life, just smaller. The next page shows how you can use a map's scale to figure out distances, and compare how big two places are.

The scale on Lee's map shows that 1 inch equals 50 kilometers. Lee wants to figure out how far across the entire continent of Australia is. He finds a piece of paper and traces out 1 inch on it so he can add up how many inches it takes to get all the way across Australia. He measures almost 80 inches across the continent at its widest point.

1. How many kilometers does that represent?

Lee isn't really sure how big that is, because he's not used to measuring distance in kilometers. He wants to convert the distance to miles, which he understands. Here's the information he needs to know:

1 mile = 1.61 kilometers
1 kilometer = .621 miles

2. How many miles across is Australia?

The United States is about 3,000 miles across from east to west in the middle of the country.

3. Is the United States wider than Australia? If so, by how many miles?

Lee also has another map. This one is of Sydney. On the Sydney map, the scale is 1 inch for every 2.5 kilometers. Lee measures about 24 inches across the widest part of Sydney, which stretches out far past the downtown area.

4. Do you think the Sydney map shows more details or fewer?

5. How many kilometers wide is Sydney, according to Lee's measurement? How many miles wide is it?

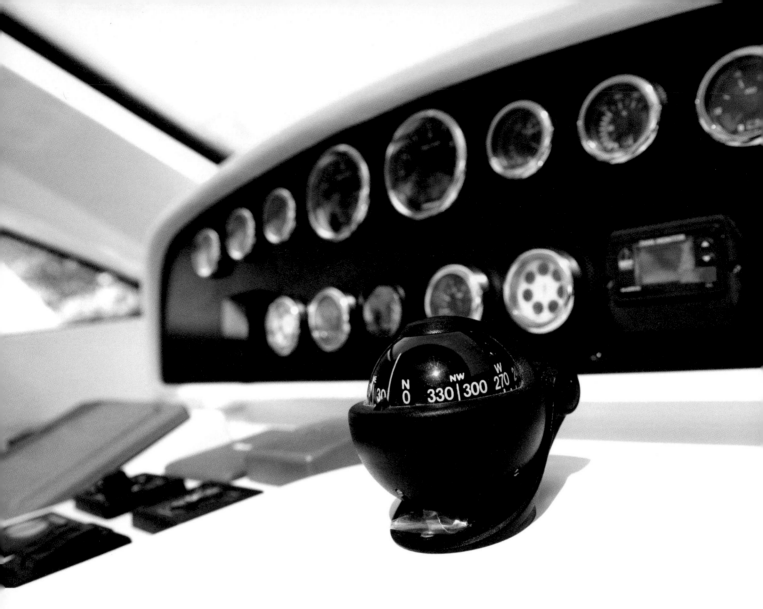

12
BOAT MATH

When Lee and his family arrive at the snorkeling business, they change into bathing suits, get their snorkeling gear, and step onto the boat. Their captain will be taking them to a coral reef about a half-hour away. Lee has ridden on planes, trains, buses, and cars so far during this trip. Now he gets to add a boat to the list!

As they sail to the reef, Lee asks the captain some questions. He wants to know how fast the boat is going. The captain tells him that boat speeds aren't measured in miles per hour or kilometers per hour. They're measured in knots, a special unit just for boat speeds. He explains how to calculate just how fast they're going, which you can do on the next page.

One knot equals 1 nautical mile per hour. That isn't helpful, though, unless you know how far a nautical mile is!

1 nautical mile = 1.151 miles per hour = 1.852 kilometers per hour

Here are the different speeds they go throughout their journey to the reef. Finish filling in the chart with miles per hour and kilometers per hour.

Time	Knots	Miles per hour	Kilometers per hour
1	9	10.36	16.67
2	13		
3	15		
4	16		
5	8		

1. What was the fastest the boat got in kilometers per hour?

2. What was the average speed in knots at which the boat traveled?

The captain tells Lee the speedboat can go up to 30 knots. On the snorkeling trips, they have to go more slowly because of the passengers, and because they don't want to accidentally damage any coral reefs under the water.

3. What is that speed in miles per hour? What about kilometers per hour?

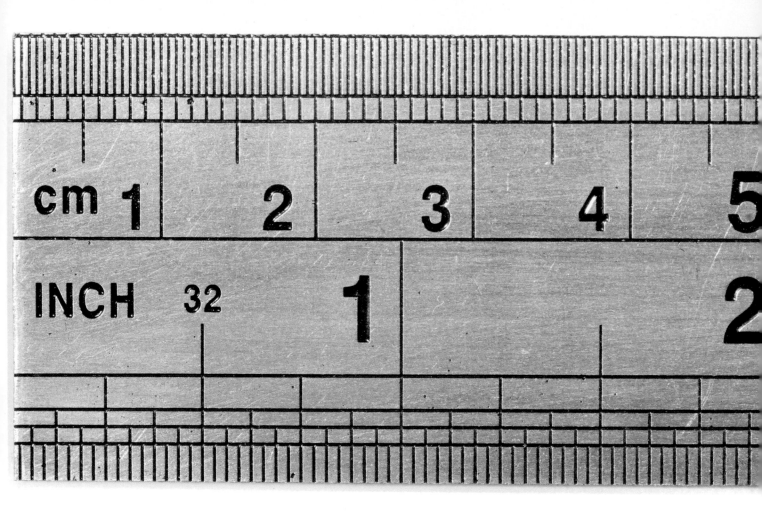

13
CONVERTING MORE MEASUREMENTS

Lee certainly has seen a lot of measurements he isn't used to. Before he traveled, he figured everyone used miles, pounds, and American dollars. Now that he's visited another country, though, he sees that different people use different measurements. For example, Australians use different types of measurements for distance, weight, temperature, and more. They use the **metric** system. In the United States, people use the U.S. Customary System, also called U.S. Standard Units.

At first, Lee was confused, but now he's figuring it out. He's trying to keep track of all the different measurements so he can keep them all straight. See what he has discovered on the next pages.

Here are some of the measurements and their conversions Lee has discovered. The first conversion in each pair is from metric to U.S. measurements.

DISTANCE
1 kilometer = .621 miles
1 mile = 1.61 kilometers

1 centimeter = .394 inches
1 inch = 2.54 centimeters

VOLUME
1 litre = .264 gallons
1 gallon = 3.79 litres

WEIGHT
1 gram = 0.035 ounces
1 ounce = 28.35 grams

1 kilogram = 2.20 pounds
1 pound = .454 kilograms

TEMPERATURE
Celsius = (Fahrenheit – 32) x 5/9
Fahrenheit = (Celsius x 9/5) + 32

1. Practice some more with measurement conversions:

   76 kilograms =
   5 gallons =
   55 degrees Fahrenheit =
   2 inches =
   52.5 kilometers =

2. Which is bigger? Insert >, =, or < in each blank below.

   30 degrees Celsius _____ 30 degrees Fahrenheit
   7.75 centimeters _____ 4 inches
   2 pounds _____ .908 kilograms
   89 ounces_____ 27 grams
   1.5 litres _____ 1 gallon

14
TOTAL TRIP COST

Lee has reached the end of his vacation in Australia. He feels like he just got there! He and his family did a lot during there vacation time, and they had a wonderful time. They ate, snorkeled, went to museums, shopped, and more.

They collect all their receipts from their vacation. Lee's mom and dad want to see how much they spent, and compare it to the budget they made before they left. How did they do? Check the next page to find out.

Everyone finds their receipts and sorts them into categories. The following is a summary of all their receipts:

hotel room: $1220
food: A$516
nice dinner: A$86
snorkeling: A$75
museum: A$32
transportation: A$178
plane tickets: $5809.30

All of these prices are in Australian dollars, except for the plane tickets and the hotel room, which they bought ahead of time while they were still in the United States.

1. Fill out this chart again, converting all the prices to American dollars.
    hotel room: $1220
    food:
    nice dinner:
    snorkeling:
    museum:
    transportation:
    plane tickets: $5809.30

Take a look at their original estimate of how much they would spend in section 2.

2. Did they stay under budget? If so, by how much? If not, how much more money than their budget allowed did they spend?

Lee also has his own receipts for things he bought with his own money. His receipts look like this:

t-shirt: $23.99
postcards: $3.50
poster: $16
snacks: $9.75

He originally had $80, which he exchanged for Australian money at the airport. Turn to section 6 for the amount of Australian money he got.

3. Did Lee end up having to exchange more money, or did he stick to his original amount? If not, how much did he have left by the end of the trip?

15
PUTTING IT ALL TOGETHER

Lee has seen and done a lot on his vacation. He's learned a lot of math, from how to convert between measurements to exchanging money to calculating distances on maps. See if you can remember some of what he has learned and done on his trip to Australia.

1. If an airline offers a discount of 8% when you buy 4 or more tickets at once, how much would you pay for 4 tickets at $630 each?

2. Can you bring a suitcase that is 24 inches long, 13 inches wide, and 8 inches tall as a carry-on? Why or why not?

3. The time zone where your friend lives is 4 hours behind where you live. What time is it there when it is 10:00 AM where you live?

   Would that be a good time to call your friend on the phone? Why or why not?

4. You are traveling to a country where the exchange rate is .89 for the U.S. dollar. How much of the other country's money would you get if you exchanged 90 U.S. dollars?

   If the exchange business you were using charges a fee of 12%, how much money would you get?

5. How much will a car cost if you rent it at $35.99 for 2 days, and pay $15 for insurance?

6. Your family's car gets an average gas mileage of 32 miles per gallon. If your family drives 290 miles, how much gas would the car use?

   Will you need to refill the gas tank if it holds 11 gallons? If not, how many more miles will it take before the gas tank is empty?

7. The scale on a map you are looking at is 1.5 inches = 10 miles. How many miles across is the area you're looking at if it is 15 inches across?

8. What is the temperature in Celsius if it is 78 degrees Fahrenheit?

Find Out More in Books

Dutta, Pia Awal. *Travel Math*. Salt Lake City, Utah: Benchmark Books, 2008.

Einspruch, Andrew. *Using Decimals to Plan Our Vacation*. North Mankato, Minn.: Capstone Press, 2010.

Marrewa, Jennifer. *How Far Away? Comparing Trips*. Milwaukee, Wisc.: Weekly Reader Early Learning, 2008.

Saddleback Educational Publishing. *21st Century Lifeskills Handbook: Transportation and Travel*. Costa Mesa, Calif.: Saddleback Publishing, 2012.

Walsh, Kieran. *Travel Math*. Vero Beach, Fla.: Rourke Publishing, 2004.

Find Out More on the Internet

Conversion Calculator
www.infoplease.com/pages/unitconversion.html

CoolMath: Geography Games
www.coolmath-games.com/1-geography-games-01.html

Math Journey
www.quia.com/mathjourney.html

Plane Math
www.planemath.com

Travel Math Trip Calculator
www.travelmath.com

Glossary

Checked: given to the airlines to put in a separate compartment in the plane.

Convert: change to.

Currency: a form of money, such as dollars, pesos, etc.

Data: information, often in number form.

Express: show or convey.

Fee: money paid for the use of a service.

Gauge: an instrument or tool used to measure the amount of something.

Hemisphere: one half of the Earth, divided either north and south or east and west.

Insurance: guarantee of payment for a loss.

Layover: a stop at an airport between two flights in which passengers must change planes.

Metric: a system of measurement based on the meter.

Proportional: corresponding in size or amount; having the same ratio as.

Rate: the speed at which something happens.

Scale: a range of values used to measure.

Transfer: to change from one plane or train to another.

Units: quantities of measurement.

Answers

1.

1. One-stop
2. Non-stop, because you don't have to add in extra time during the layover.
3. $1651.79 – $1639.80 = $11.99
4. $412.95
5. $1651.79 – $412.95 = $1238.84
6. $1238.84 + $1238.84 + $1651.79 + $1651.79 = $5781.26

2.

1. Hotel room: $1225
   Food: $480
   Nice dinner: $100
   Snorkeling: $80
   Beach: $0
   Museum: $34
   Transportation: $300
2. $2219; $8000.26
3. No, they don't have enough yet; they will need to save $412.51 more.
4. $540.55/4 = $103.13

3.

1. 57 inches; yes
2. Jeans, video game, and magazine OR hiking boots and extra shirt OR jeans and shirt, etc.
3. The second one.

4.

1. 5:30 PM + 1:30 = 7:00 PM
2. 7:00 PM + 3:30 = 10:30 PM
3. 10:30 PM – 2:00 = 8:30 PM
4. 8:30 PM – 18 hours = 2:30 AM on Monday

5.

1. 504 mph
2. 502 mph; it is a little lower because you didn't account for the takeoff and landing speeds in your first average, which are slower than cruise speed.

6.

1. A$76
2. .1 x $80 = $8, $80 – $8 = $72
3. $72 x .95 = A$68.4
4. $50 x .1 = $5, $50 – $5 = $45, $45 x .95 = $42.75
5. $100 x .1 = $10, $100 – $10 = $90, $90 ÷ .95 = $94.74

7.

1. No
2. The 10:07 (9:35 + 27 = 10:01)
3. Yes, they will wait for 6 minutes.
4. 10:07 + :16 + :04 = 10:27

8.

1. $39.90, $53.90, and $71.90
2. $53.90 + $11 + $15 = $79.90
3. 22.5 miles (38 + 38 + 1.5 = 77.5, 100 – 77.5 = 22.5)
4. Yes, by 7.5 miles; they will have to pay $.75

9.

1. 77.5/6 = 12.92 miles/litre
2. 7.72 litres/100 kilometers
3. 6 litres x 137.9 cents = 827.4 cents = $8.27

10.

1. 18 miles/(12.92 miles/litre) = 1.39 litres; 1.39 litres x 137.9 = 191.7 = $1.92
2. $10 +$1.92 = $11.92
3. $2.50 x 4 x 2 = $20

4. 45 minutes; 58 minutes
5. They should drive, because it is cheaper and faster.

11.

1. About 4,000 kilometers
2. 4,000 kilometers x .621 miles = 2,484 miles.
3. Yes, by about 516 miles.
4. More details
5. About 60 kilometers, or 37.26 miles

12.

1. 29.62 kilometers per hour
2. 12.2 knots
3. 34.53 miles per hour; 55.56 kilometers per hour

Time	Knots	Miles per hour	Kilometers per hour
1	9	10.36	16.67
2	13	14.96	24.08
3	15	17.27	27.78
4	16	18.42	29.63
5	8	9.21	14.82

13.

1. 76 kilograms = 167.2 pounds
   5 gallons = 18.95 litres
   55 degrees Fahrenheit = 12.78 degrees Celsius
   2 inches = 5.08 centimeters
   52.5 kilometers = 32.6 miles

2. >
   <
   =
   >
   <

14.

1. Hotel room: $1220
   Food: $543.16
   Nice dinner: $90.53
   Snorkeling: $78.95
   Museum: $33.68
   Transportation: $187.37
   Plane tickets: $5809.30
2. They stayed under budget by $37.27 ($8000.26 – $7962.99 = $37.27)
3. He didn't have to exchange more money; he has $15.16 left ($68.40 –53.24)

15.

1. $630 x 4 = $2520, $2520 x .08 = $201.60, $2520 – $201.60 = $2318.40
2. No, because the length is over the limit.
3. 6:00 AM; No, because your friend would be sleeping.
4. $90 x .89 = $80.10; $70.49 (.12 x $90 = $10.80, $90 – $10.80 = $79.20, $79.20 x .89 = $70.49)
5. $86.98
6. 290/32 = 9.06; Not yet; 1.94 gallons x 32 miles/gallon = 62.08 miles left
7. 100 miles (15 inches/1.5 inches = 10, 10 x 10 miles = 100 miles)
8. 25.56

INDEX

ABOUT THE AUTHOR

Helen Thompson lives in upstate New York. She worked first as a social worker and then became a teacher as her second career.

Picture Credits

Dreamstime.com:

AUG - - 2014